Mel Bay Presents

101 EASY Fingerstyle Guitar Solos

by Larry McCabe

CD Contents

1 2 3 4 5 6 7 8 9 0

Visit us on the Web at www.melbay.com — E-mail us at email@melbay.com

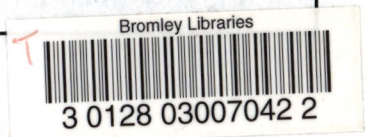

CONTENTS

INTRODUCTION

Welcome to Mel Bay's *101 Easy Fingerstyle Guitar Solos.* This book contains a wealth of time-honored songs that have been played and enjoyed by many generations of musicians. Many styles are covered here: children's songs, Christmas songs, American standards, hymns and spirituals, blues, calypso, train songs, Stephen Foster songs, patriotic songs, and more. The arrangements are designed for beginning to intermediate guitar players, and can be played on classical, electric, and steel-string acoustic guitars.

You are sure to find some of your old favorites here, and I am confident that you will discover some "new favorites" as well. We hope this book becomes a good friend and companion to you and your guitar in the years to come.

HOW TO USE THIS BOOK

The Written Music

Each example is written in both notation and tablature exactly as it is recorded.

Fingerings

1. Suggested fretting-hand fingerings are provided in the notation staff. The recommended fingerings are not absolute, and you may modify a particular fingering if you have a better idea.

1 = First (index) finger   2 = Second (middle) finger   3 = Third (ring) finger   4 = Fourth (little) finger

2. Individual approaches to picking-hand fingering vary greatly; for instance, classical guitarists often use a different technique than a blues guitarist. Most of the arrangements in this book leave the picking-hand fingering up to the player.

The Companion CD

1. An "A" tuning note is provided on the first track of the companion CD.

2. Most of the songs have their own CD track. Because the current technology allows only 99 tracks, a few tracks contain two songs. For your convenience, each doubled track contain short songs.

Procedure

The songs are arranged in alphabetical order rather than by degree of difficulty (degree of difficulty is sometimes a subjective issue). Feel free to work through the songs in any order. If you encounter an arrangement that is too difficult, try another song, and then return to the more challenging arrangement later.

Abilene

American Folk Song

9780786657933

Chorus

Abilene, Abilene,
Prettiest town I ever seen;
Folks out there don't treat you mean
In Abilene, my Abilene.

Crowded city, ain't nothin' free,
Ain't nothin' in this town for me;
Wish to the Lord that I could be
In Abilene, my Abilene.

Sit alone every night,
Watch the trains run out of sight;
Don't I wish they were carrying me to
Abilene, my Abilene.

Across the Western Ocean

Irish Sea Chantey

All the Good Times Are Past and Gone

TRACK 4

Old-time and Bluegrass Song

All the Pretty Little Horses

TRACK 5

African Lullaby

Au Clair De La Lune

TRACK 6

French Folksong

Shift to the third position for the D7 chord in measure 11

Aura Lee

Minstrel Song, 1861

This melody was used for Elvis Presley's "Love Me Tender" in 1956.

The Banks of the Ohio

TRACK 8

American Folksong

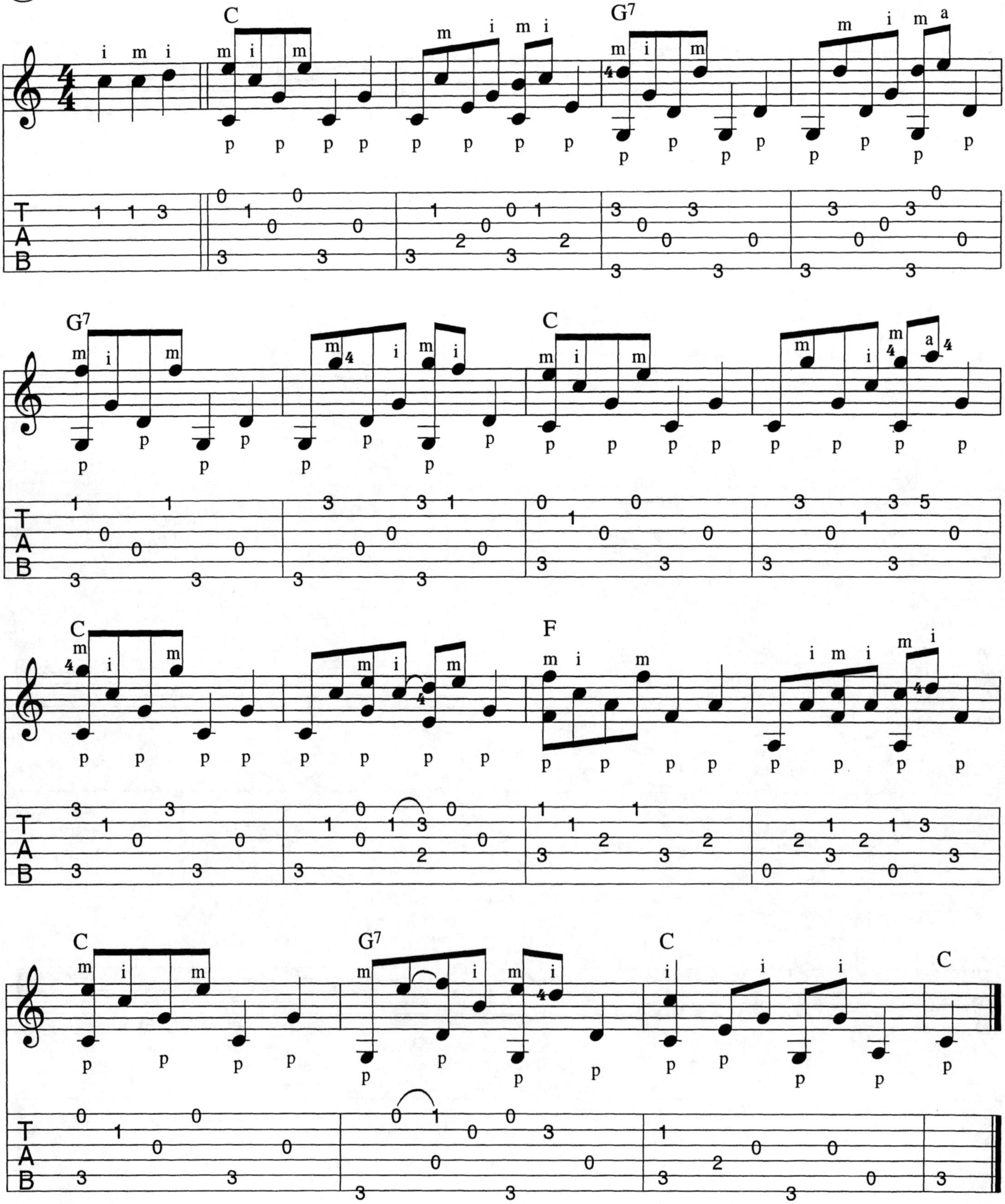

Big Ball in Boston

Traditional Country

Also known as "Big Ball in Nashville," Big Ball in Cowtown," "Big Ball in Bristol,"
etc. Played by old-time country, bluegrass, and Western Swing musicians.

Tip re: measure seven: Non-classical guitarists often fret the F♯ (6th string) with the thumb of
the fretting hand.

Chorus

Big ball in Boston, big ball in town;
Big ball in Boston, we'll dance around.

Let's have a party, let's have a time;
Let's have a party, I won't need a dime.

Roll on the ground, boys, roll on the ground;
Eat salty crackers, ten cents a pound.

My love's in jail, boys, my love's in jail;
My love's in jail, boys, who'll go her bail?

Bile Them Cabbage Down

Called "Boil Them Cabbage Down" by folks who are grammatically correct.

Comic Folk Song

Blow the Wind Southerly

TRACK 11

Traditional English

The Blue Bell of Scotland

Dorothea Bland Jordan
Scotland ca. 1800

Bury Me Beneath the Willow

TRACK 13

American Folksong

Bury Me Not on the Lone Prairie

Based on the poem "The Ocean Burial" by E.H. Chapin, 1839
Music by George N. Allen, 1849

TRACK 14

Camptown Races

The original title of this well-known Foster song: "Gwine To Run All Night.'

Stephen Foster
Minstrel Song, 1850

Careless Love

TRACK 16

Folk Blues

One of the earliest blues songs, "Careless Love" first appeared in print in 1911 as "Kelly's Love.'

Clementine

TRACK 17

Barker Bradford, c. 1884

Corrine, Corrina

Blues

This blues standard has been recorded by many diverse artists, incluing jazz trumpeter Red Nichols, Western Swing band leader Bob Wills, and blues guitarist Taj Mahal.

Cripple Creek

TRACK 19

Old-time Tune

The best version I have heard of this song was by the late David Akeman,
the great singer and old-time banjo player whose stage name was "Stringbean."

Verse

Chorus

Well, the easiest money that ever I made,
I made up in Cripple Creek layin' in the shade;
Girls up in Cripple Creek about half grown,
Jump on a man like a dog on a bone.

Chorus
Goin' up Cripple Creek, goin' at a run;
Goin' up Cripple Creek to have a little fun.
Goin' up Cripple Creek, goin' at a run,
Goin' up Cripple Creek to have a little fun.

I got a gal at the head of the creek,
Goin' up to see her in the middle of the week;
Goin' up Cripple Creek, goin' in a wiz,
Goin' up Cripple Creek to see little Liz.

Cripple Creek's wide and Cripple Creek's deep,
I'll wade old Cripple Creek 'fore I sleep;
Roll my britches up to my knees,
I'll wade old Cripple Creek when I please.

The Cruel War

Traditional

Peter, Paul and Mary sang a beautiful arrangement of "The Cruel War" back in the '60s.
The song goes slowly, with lots of feeling.

The cruel war is raging,	Your captain will call you,	Oh, Johnny, oh Johnny,
Johnny has to fight;	It grieves my heart so;	I fear you are unkind;
I want to be with him	Won't you let me go with you?	I love you far better
From morning till night.	No, my love no.	Than all of mankind.
I want to be with him,	I'll tie back my hair,	I love you far better
It grieves my heart so;	Men's clothing I'll put on;	Than words can e'er express;
Won't you let me go with you?	I'll pass as your comrade	Won't you let me go with you?
No, my love no.	As we march along.	Yes, my love yes.
Tomorrow is Sunday,	I'll pass as your comrade,	
And Monday is the day	No one will ever know;	
When your captain will call you,	Won't you let me go with you?	
And you must obey.	No, my love no.	

Danville Girl

American Folk Song

Down in the Valley

American Folk Song

For an easier version, play only the first bass note in each measure.

Drunken Sailor

Sea Chantey

24

East Virginia

TRACK 24

Traditional

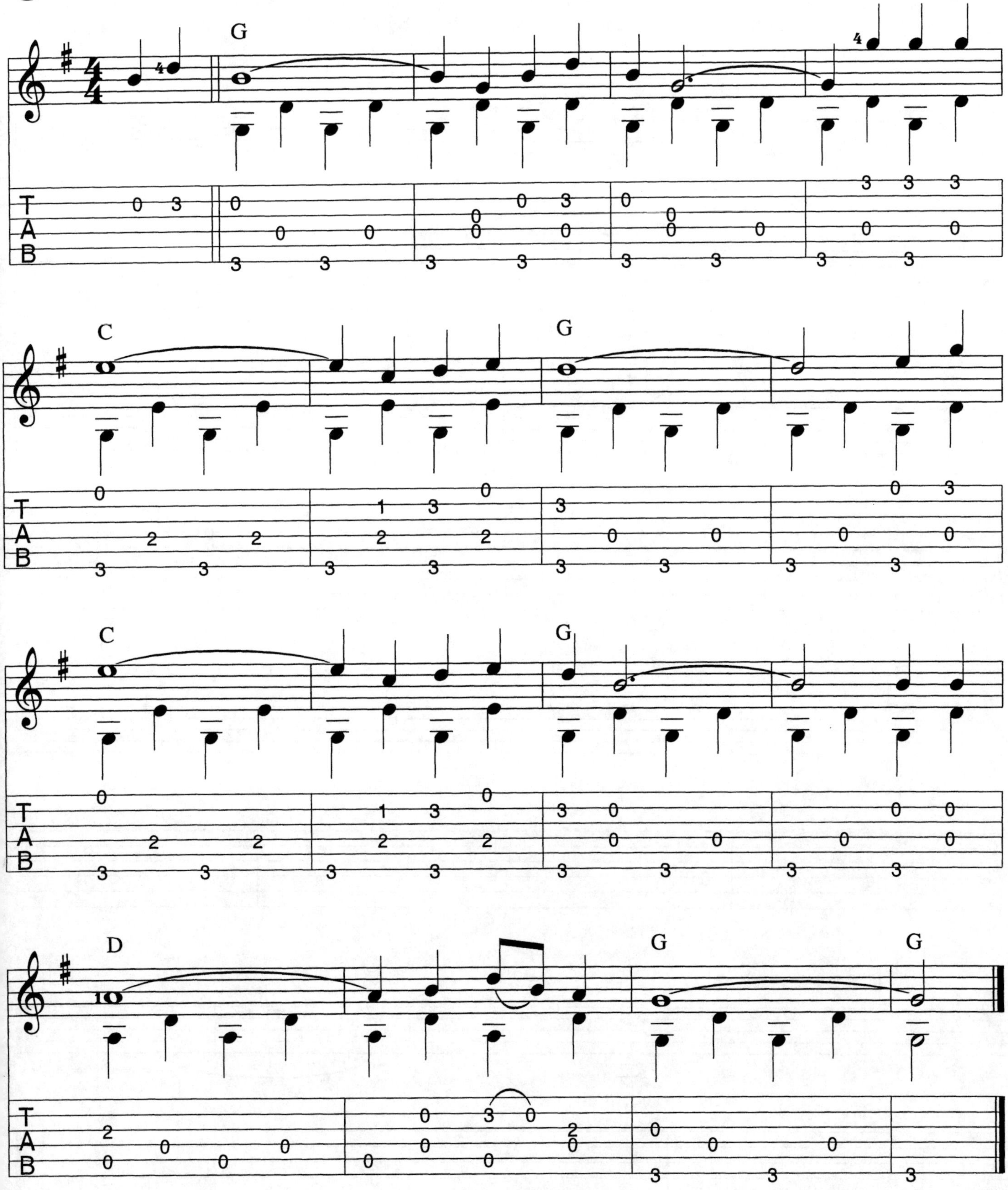

Fair Eleanor

English Folk Song

A tragic romance in the English ballad tradition. Fair Eleanor's heart was
pierced by a knife-wielding rival, who was in turn put to death by Eleanor's
true love, Lord Thomas.

Faith of Our Fathers

Words by Frederick Faber
Music by H.F. Hemy, 1864

TRACK 26

Frankie and Johnny

American Blues Song

Barrelhouse piano style - "swing" the eighth notes.

Freight Train

Fingerpicking Standard

God Is So Good

African Gospel Song

The melody is in the lower voice and is written with down stems. Notes with
up stems are accompanying notes. Play the melody louder than the accompaniment.

Good Night, Ladies

Words by E.P. Christie, 1847

30

Green Grow the Lilacs

Traditional

Variation: Change the rhythm of some or all of the quarter-note melody measures to the following: dotted quarter, eighth, quarter note.

Groundhog

Mountain Song

Arranged in bluegrass banjo style. Melody notes are indicated by accent marks.

Hand Me Down My Walking Cane

American Folk Song

Handsome Molly

Traditional

I wish I were in London	Don't you remember, Molly,	Her hair was black as a raven,
Or some other seaport town;	You gave me your right hand?	Her eyes as black as coal;
I'd set my foot in a steamboat,	You said if ever you'd marry	Her cheeks they was like lilies
I'd sail the ocean 'round.	That I would be your man.	Out in the morning cold.
While sailing 'round the ocean,	You rode to church last Sunday,	I'll go down to the river
While sailing round the sea;	You passed me right on by;	When everyone's asleep;
I'd think of Handsome Molly	I know your mind is changin'	I'll think of Handsome Molly
Wherever she may be.	By the rovin' of your eye.	Then lay me down to weep.

34

The House of the Rising Sun

Folk Blues

BV----------------¬ Symbol for *barre chord.* Cover three or more strings with the first finger at the fret indicated by the Roman numeral.

Allow the melody notes (stems down) to ring while softly playing the accompanying arpeggios.

35

Hush, Little Baby

TRACK 36

Lullaby

This well-known children's song has been rearranged and recorded
under the title "Mockingbird" by several rock singers.

Hush, little baby, don't say a word,
Papa'a gonna buy you a mockingbird;
And if that mockingbird don't sing,
Papa's gonna buy you a diamond ring.

And if that diamond ring is brass,
Papa's gonna buy you a looking glass;
And if that looking glass gets broke,
Papa's gonna buy you a billy goat.

And if that billy goat don't pull,
Papa's gonna buy you a cart and bull;
And if that cart and bull turn over,
Papa's gonna buy you a dog named Rover.

And if that dog named Rover won't bark,
Papa's gonna buy you a horse and cart;
And if that horse and cart break down,
You'll still be the prettiest girl in town.

I Know Where I'm Going

Traditional Irish

"I Know Where I'm Going" blends simplicity of form (an 8-bar
verse) with the beautiful, misty sound that is typical of Irish airs.

I know where I'm going,
And I know who's going with me;
I know who I love,
But the Lord knows who I'll marry.

I have stockings of silk,
Shoes of fine green leather;
Combs to buckle my hair,
And a ring on every finger.

Some say he's black,
But I say he's bonnie;
The fairest of them all
Is my handsome, winsome Johnny.

Feather beds are soft,
And painted rooms are bonnie;
But I would trade them all
For my handsome, winsome Johnny.

I know where I'm going,
And I know who's going with me;
I know who I love,
And my dear knows who I'll marry.

I'm on My Way

Gospel Song

It Ain't Gonna Rain No More

Traditional

I Wish I Was Single Again

Minstrel Song

" . . . and if I were single, my pockets would jingle . . ."

J'ai Passe Devant ta Porte

Cajun Waltz

Johnny Get Your Haircut

Traditional Folk Song

Johnny get your haircut,
Haircut, haircut;
Johnny get your haircut,
Just like me!

41

Johnny Has Gone For a Soldier

Song of the American Revolution

This lament describes the effects of war from a woman's point of view. Popular at the time of the Revolution–and revived during the Civil War–the melody is of Irish origin.

Here I sit on Buttermilk Hill,
Who could blame me, cry my fill;
And every tear would turn a mill,
Johnny has gone for a soldier.

My oh my, I loved him so,
Broke my heart to see him go;
And only time will heal my woe,
Johnny has gone for a soldier.

I'll sell my flax, I'll sell my wheel,
Buy my love a sword of steel;
So it in battle he may wield,
Johnny has gone for a soldier.

I'll dye my petticoat, I'll dye it red,
And 'round the world I'll beg my bread;
For the lad I love from me has fled,
Johnny has gone for a soldier.

42

Jolly Old Saint Nicholas

Christmas Song

The thumb (Th.) is used to fret bass notes in measures 5, 8, 13, and 15.

The Joys of Love
(Plaisir D' Amour)

TRACK 45

John Paul Martini
French Song

Just As I Am

Words by Charlotte Elliot ca. 1835
Music ("Woodworth") by William Bradbury, 1849

TRACK 46

Kevin Barry

TRACK 47

Ireland

Kevin Barry, an eighteen-year old Irish freedom fighter, was hanged
by the British in the Mountjoy Jail, Dublin, on November 1, 1920.

Chorus

Early on a Monday morning,	**"Shoot me like an Irish soldier,**	Just before he faced the hangman
High upon a gallows tree;	**Do not hang me like a dog;**	In his lonely prison cell;
Kevin Barry gave his young life	**For I fought to free old Ireland**	British soldiers tortured Barry,
For the cause of liberty.	**On that dark September morn."**	Just because he wouldn't tell.
Just a lad of eighteen summers,	"All around that little bakery	
Still there's no one can deny;	Where we fought them hand to hand;	Another martyr for old Ireland,
As he walked to death that morning	Shoot me like an Irish soldier,	Another murder for the Crown;
Nobly held his head up high.	For I fought to free Ireland."	Brutal laws to crush the Irish
		Could not keep their spirits down.

Little Rosewood Casket

TRACK 48

Traditional

Barre the four top strings at the
2nd fret (EBGD) for two beats.

Liza Jane

TRACK 49

Traditional Folk Song

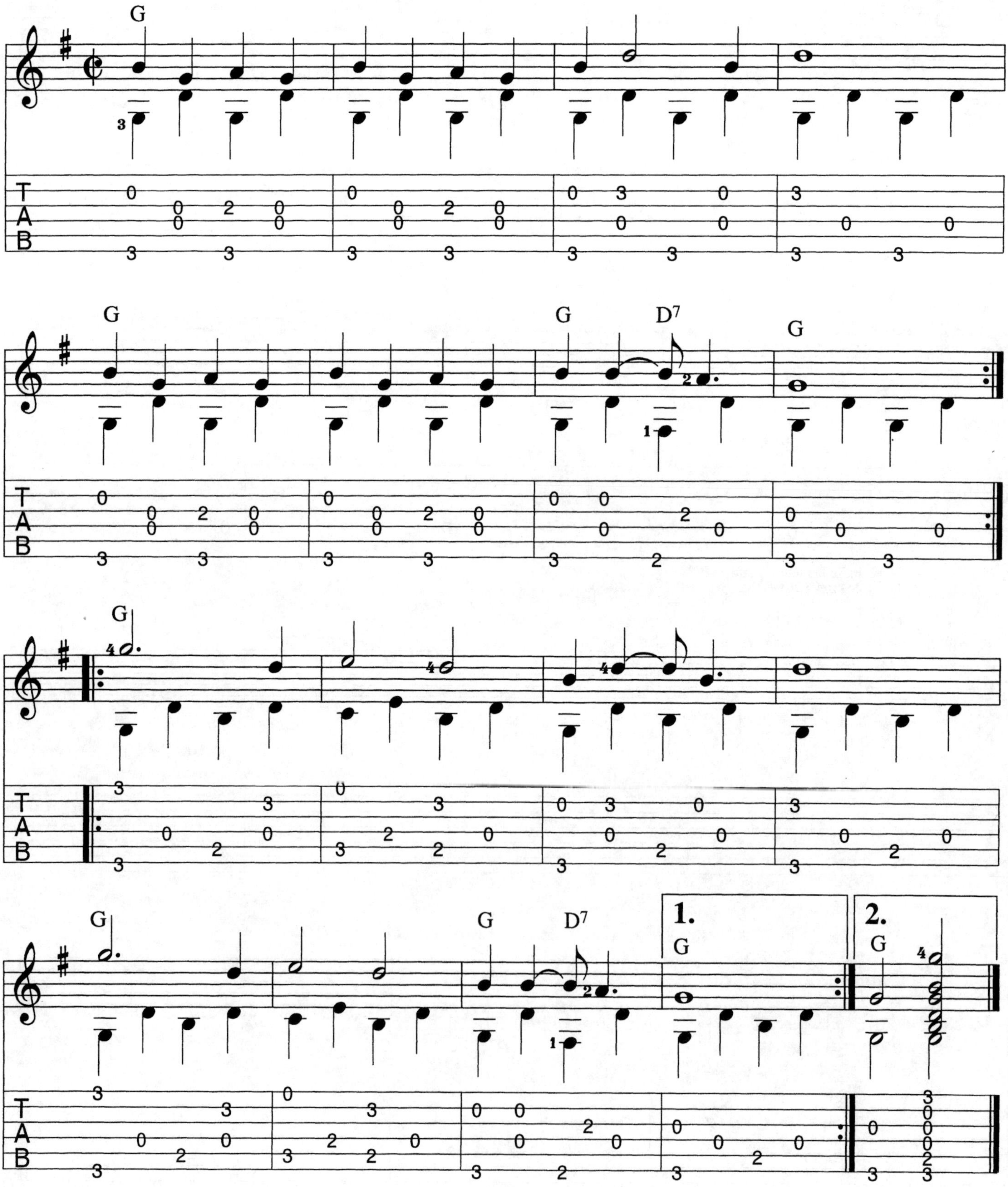

Loch Lomond
(You Take the High Road)

TRACK 50

Traditional Scottish

Lonesome Valley
(You've Got to Walk That Lonesome Valley)

Spiritual

Long Journey Home

TRACK 52

Folk and Bluegrass Song

Also known as "Two Dollar Bill" ("Lost all my money but a two-dollar bill . . .").

Look Down That Lonesome Road

TRACK 53

Spiritual, ca 1865

Lord Randall

England

The traditional British ballad, "Lord Randall," ("Where have you been, Lord Randall, my son?") was almost certainly the foundation for Bob Dylan's "A Hard Rain's Gonna Fall."

Love Came Down at Christmas

TRACK 55

Irish Christmas Carol

Mary Ann

Traditional Calypso Song

Mary Hamilton

English Ballad

Midnight Special

Huddie Ledbetter ("Leadbelly") first brought this old prison song to the attention of the general public back in 1941. Since then, "Midnight Special" has been recorded by many artists including Harry Belafonte, Johnny Rivers, and Creedence Clearwater Revival.

Chorus

Sing three times: Let the Midnight Special shine her light on me,
                    Let the Midnight Special shine her everlovin' light on me.

Midst the Deep Silence

TRACK 59

Polish Christmas Carol

Mississippi Delta Blues

Play very slowly, with a blues shuffle feel.

Moderato

TRACK 61

Maurio Giuliani

Ring finger plays first string.   Middle finger plays second string.
First finger plays third string.   Thumb plays the bass strings (4-5-6).

Carlo Mario Giuliani (1781-1828)
Self-taught guitar virtuoso; lived in Vienna 1807-1819; aquaintance of Beethoven; toured Russia and England, then settled in Naples. Composer of more than 200 tunes for the guitar.

Molly Malone

TRACK 62

Traditional Irish Ballad

New River Train

Bluegrass

Nine Hundred Miles

Traditional Folk Song

Nine-Pound Hammer

Kentucky Coal Mining Song

November

TRACK 66

Bohemian Folk Song

Oh, Mary Don't You Weep

TRACK 67

Spiritual

Old Joe Clark

Traditional Hoedown

Pay Me My Money Down

Calypso

Chorus
Pay me, oh, pay me,
  Pay me my money down;
Pay me or go to jail,
  Pay me my money down.

I thought I heard the captain say,
  Pay me my money down;
Tomorrow is our sailing day,
  Pay me my money down.   (Chorus)

The very next day we cleared the bar,
  Pay me my money down;
He knocked me down with the end of a spar,
  Pay me my money down.   (Chorus)

I wish I was Mr. Howard's son,
  Pay me my money down;
Sit in the house and drink good rum,
  Pay me my money down.   (Chorus)

I wish I was Mr. Steven's son,
  Pay me my money down;
Sit on the bank and watch all the work done,
  Pay me my money down.   (Chorus)

Poor Ellen Smith

Traditional

Poor Ellen Smith,
How she was found;
Shot through the heart
Lying cold on the ground.

Her clothes were all scattered
And thrown on the ground;
And blood marks the spot
Where poor Ellen was found.

Saw her on a Monday
Before that sad day;
They found her poor body
And took it away.

Who had the heart,
Who had the face;
To murder my sweetheart
In this lonesome place?

I laid out six months
And prayed all the time;
They might find the one
That committed the crime.

Now I'm in jail
And God knows it's hard;
While my sweet Ellen
Sleeps in the graveyard.

The warden just told me
That soon I'll be free;
To go to her grave
Near that old willow tree.

The jury will hang me,
That is, if they can;
But Lord knows I'll die
As an innocent man.

Prelude in C

M. Carcassi

Pretty Polly

TRACK 72

Appalachian Mountains

The melody is indicated by notes with down stems.
Play slowly and mournfully.

Railroad Bill

Traditional

Railroad Bill, Railroad Bill,
He never worked and he never will;
And it's ride, old Railroad Bill.

Railroad Bill was a mighty bad man,
Shot the light from the brakeman's hand:
And it's ride, old Railroad Bill.

Railroad Bill goin' over the hill,
Lightin' cigars with a ten-dollar bill;
And it's ride, old Railroad Bill.

Railroad Bill was mighty bad,
He shot his ma and beat up his dad;
And it's ride, old Railroad Bill.

Four policemen dressed in blue,
Come around the corner two by two;
And it's ride, old Railroad Bill.

Railroad Bill, before he died,
Said he'd build a train for all the hoboes to ride;
And it's ride, old Railroad Bill.

Rain

French Folk Song

FINGERPICKING TIPS

The bass patterns shown below can be used in many songs in this book. Some of these patterns are fairly challenging, but patience and persistence always yields results.

• Steel-string guitarists often fret the F bass note (Ex. 2-3) with the thumb.
• Likewise, steel-string guitarists commonly fret the F# bass note (Ex. 4-5) with the thumb.

The Riddle Song

British Isles

Ring the Banjo

Stephen Foster
Minstrel Song, 1851

TRACK 76

Rock My Soul

Spiritual ca.1830

"Rock My Soul" is one of the great rocking, rafter-shaking spirituals of the Antebellum era. The influence of this type of song can be heard on the recordings of Mahalia Jackson, Sam Cooke, Aretha Franklin, and many of today's leading gospel singers.

Rock my soul in the bosom of Abraham,
Rock my soul in the bosom of Abraham,
Rock my soul in the bosom of Abraham,
Oh, rock-a my soul!

So high, I can't get over it,
So low, I can't get under it,
So wide, I can't get around it,
Oh, rock-a my soul!

Roll in My Sweet Baby's Arms

TRACK 78

Bluegrass Song

Saint James' Infirmary

Blues

I went down to Saint James' Infimary,
Saw my baby there;
Stretched out on a cold white table,
So sweet, so cold, so fair.

Went up to see the doctor,
"Can't help you, son," he said;
When I went back to see my woman
She had left for another world.

Well, I tried to keep from cryin',
My heart felt just like lead;
She was all I had to live for,
I wish it was me instead,

When I die, please dress me in the new look,
With a fancy coat and a real-gone hat;
Put a twenty-caret gold ring on my finger,
And have a jazz band play the "Skit-Dee-Doo-Skat."

Salty Dog

Bluegrass Song

Sandy Land

Traditional

Scarborough Fair

Traditional English Song

Shady Grove

Traditional

Like all folk songs, "Shady Grove" has many variations. Usually the title refers to a place, but in some versions "Shady Grove" is the unusual name of an esteemed female companion.

Chorus
Shady Grove, my little love,
Shady Grove, I say;
Shady Grove, my little love,
Bound to go away.

I wish I had a big fine horse
And corn to feed him on;
And Shady Grove could stay at home
And feed him when I'm away.

Went to see my Shady Grove,
She was standin' in the door;
Her shoes and stockings in her hand
And her little bare feet on the floor.

When I was a little boy
I wanted a Barlow knife;
Now I want little Shady Grove
To say she'll be my wife.

Kiss from little Shady Grove
Is sweet as brandy wine;
And there ain't no girl in this old world
That's prettier than mine.

Short'nin' Bread

TRACK 83

Southern Song

Three little babies lyin' in bed,
Two was sick and the other 'most dead;
Sent for the doctor, doctor said,
"Give them babies short'nin' bread."

Chorus
Mammy's little baby loves short'nin, short'nin',
Mammy's little baby loves short'nin' bread.
Mammy's little baby loves short'nin', short'nin',
Mammy's little baby loves short'nin' bread.

I slipped in the kitchen, raised up the lid,
Stole me a mess of that short'nin' bread;
I wunk at the pretty gal and I said,
"Baby, how'd you like some short'nin' bread?"

They caught me with the skillet, caught me with the lid,
Caught me with the gal makin' shortnin' bread;
Six months for the skillet, six months for the lid,
Now I'm doin' time for eatin' short'nin' bread.

Sinner Man

Gospel Song

Skip to My Lou

Folk Song

The Skye Boat Song

Scottish Air

Sourwood Mountain

Appalachian Song

Spinning Wheel Song

Traditional Gaelic

Steel Mill Blues

The Streets of Laredo

Cowboy Song

Sugar Babe

Texas Blues

There's a River of Life

L. Casebolt
Hymn

TRACK 90

Tom Dooley

American Outlaw Ballad
1866

TRACK 91

"Tom Dooley" is a song based on a real crime that occurred in 1866, in the mountains of northwest North Carolina. Tom Dula, an ex-Confederate soldier who had fought with Zeb Vance's 26th regiment, was in love with both Laura Foster and her cousin Ann Melton. In 1866 Laura was stabbed to death and her body was placed in a shallow grave, where it was soon discovered. After two trials in which both Tom and Ann were tried for the crime, Dula was convicted and hanged on May 1, 1868.

At the second trial, Dula testified that Ann Melton was innocent and that he alone was guilty. Many years later, just before she died, Ann Melton confessed to being the one who had actually murdered her cousin.

This traditional folksong was popularly adapted and revived by the Kingston Trio in 1958, and the great success of the Trio's recording helped to launch the folk music revival that lasted until the mid 1960s.

I met her on the mountain,
That's where I took her life;
Met her upon the mountain,
I stabbed her with my knife.

Chorus
Hang down your head, Tom Dooley,
Hang down your head and cry;
Hang down your head, Tom Dooley,
Poor boy you're bound to die.

They're going to try Ann Melton.
Can't see no reason why;
There's only one who's guilty
And now I'm going to die.

This time tomorrow morning
This soldier boy will be
Down in a lonesome valley
Hangin' from a white oak tree.

We Three Kings of Orient Are

J.H. Hopkins Jr.
1857

TRACK 92

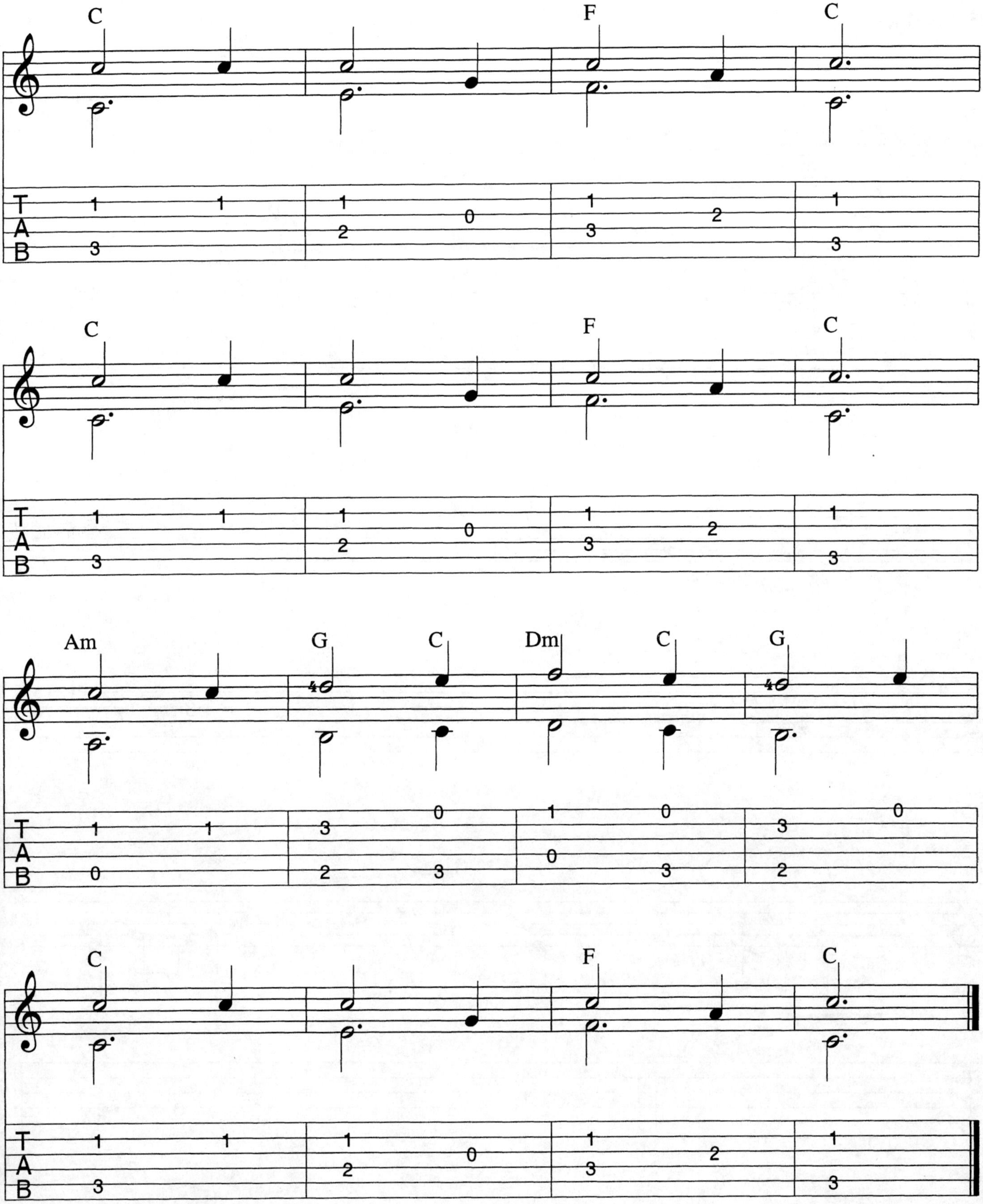
C F C
T A B
C F C
T A B
Am G C Dm C G
T A B
C F C
T A B

What a Friend We Have in Jesus

Words by Haratius Bonar
Music by Charles Converse
1876

TRACK 93

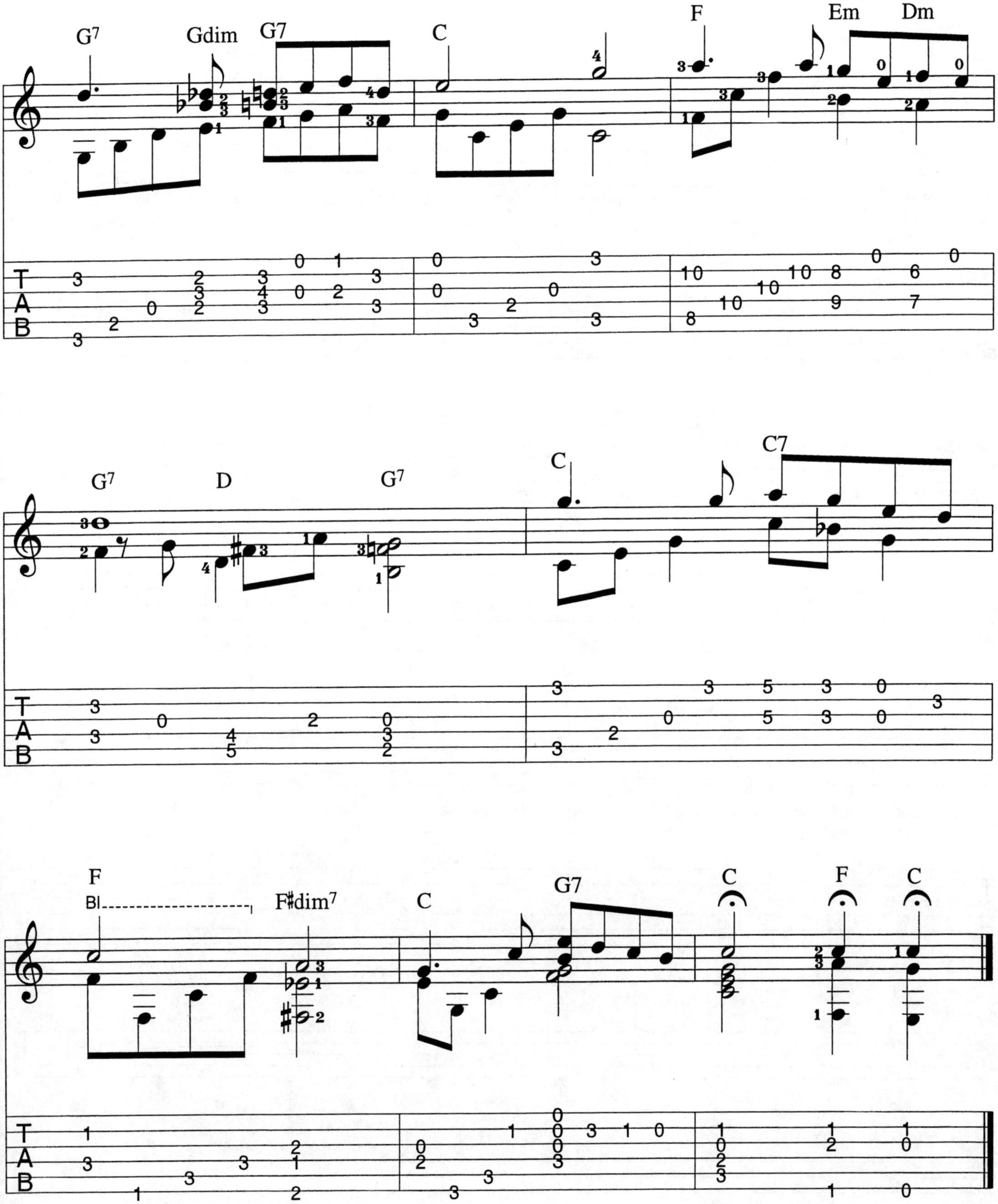
G7
Gdim
G7
C
F
Em
Dm
G7
D
G7
C
C7
F
BI
F♯dim7
C
G7
C
F
C
T
A
B

When the Saints Go Marching In

Words by Katherine E. Purvis
Music by James M. Black
New Orleans, 1896

TRACK 94

Wildwood Flower

Traditional

Will the Circle Be Unbroken

Traditional

William Taylor

Traditional English Song

Wreck of the Old '97

Hillbilly Hit Record, 1924-25

Yankee Doodle

TRACK 99

Song of the American Revolution

INDEX OF SONGS BY STYLE